My Best Book of

Ancient Rome

Deborah Murrell

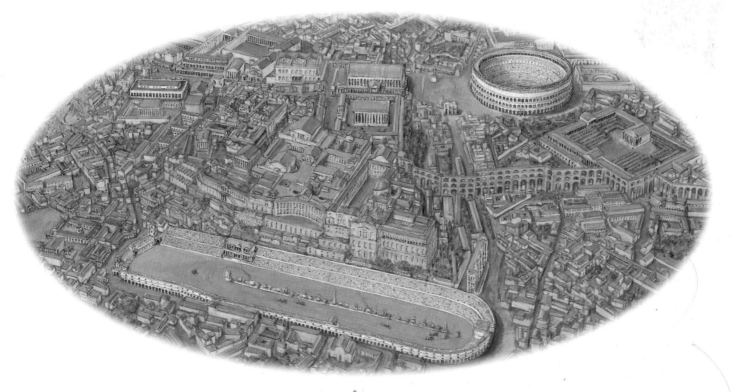

KINGFISHER

Contents

KINGFISHER

Kingfisher Publications Plc
New Penderel House
283–288 High Holborn
London WC1V 7HZ

www.kingfisherpub.com

Created for Kingfisher Publications Plc
by Picthall & Gunzi Limited

Author and editor: Deborah Murrell
Designer: Dominic Zwemmer
Consultant: Richard Platt

Illustrators: Richard Hook, Adam
Hook, Angus McBride, Simoné
Boni, Peter Dennis, Les Edwards,
Luigi Galante, David Salariya,
Ron Tiner, Thomas Trojer

First published by Kingfisher
Publications Plc 2004

10 9 8 7 6 5 4 3 2 1

1TR/0304/WKT/MAR(MAR)/128KMA

Copyright © Kingfisher
Publications Plc 2004

A CIP catalogue record for this book
is available from the British Library.

ISBN 0 7534 0958 5

Printed in China

How Rome began

Britain

France (Gaul)

Italy

Rome

Greece

About 3,000 years ago, a tribe of people called the Latins settled on the hills where Rome stands today. They had chosen a good place to live. From the top of the hills they could easily see any enemies approaching. The River Tiber below supplied fresh water, and they could reach the sea by boat. Soon, more villages grew up nearby and eventually they all joined together to form the city of Rome.

Where was early Rome?

Rome was on a fertile plain in Latium, a part of what is now Italy. To the north of Rome lived the Etruscans, and to the south lived a colony of Greek people. There were also smaller tribes of hill farmers, including the Sabines and the Samnites.

River Tiber

The hills of Rome

Rome is said to be built on seven hills. One of them, the Palatine hill, was probably the site of the first Latin villages. Later, the emperors of Rome built their grand homes there. The word 'palace' comes from the name of the Palatine hill.

The Etruscan enemy

The early Romans learned a lot from their powerful neighbours. The Greeks taught them science, architecture and the arts. The Etruscans introduced them to gladiators, chariot races and the toga. The Etruscans often attacked Rome, and by about 600BCE it was under Etruscan control. Historians believe that the last three kings of Rome were Etruscans.

Etruscan warriors attacked many Roman villages.

The Capitoline hill, below, is the centre of government in modern Rome.

Early farmers grew grains, vegetables and fruit.

Farmers used simple ploughs to prepare the land for planting.

Roman rulers

The first rulers of Rome were all kings. A group of men called senes, or senators, elected each king and advised him during his reign. According to some historians, there were seven Roman kings in total, and the last three were Etruscans, though nobody is sure. The last king, Tarquinius II, was overthrown in about 510BCE, and Rome became a republic.

Tarquin the Proud

King Tarquinius II was also known as Tarquinius Superbus, which means 'the proud'. A Roman historian called Livy said that the king was very unpopular. Eventually, the people of Rome drove the whole royal family out of the city.

Paying the price

There were 300 members of the Senate, all men from the richest families, known as patricians. Senators were expected to pay for things such as public buildings and entertaining people. Some of them spent so much that they became bankrupt!

A tribune could stop any official act by saying 'veto', meaning 'I forbid'.

People power

People who were not patricians were known as plebeians. Some plebeians felt it was unfair that only patricians could be senators. In 494BCE, they threatened to leave Rome unless changes were made. So the Senate granted them their own council with tribunes to speak for them. Later, they gained the power of veto.

Hot topics

Some Romans, such as Cicero, were great orators, or public speakers. They could win support for their side of the argument by their words alone. Debates in the Senate could become quite heated!

The senators held debates in the Senate.

Senators usually wore togas for formal occasions.

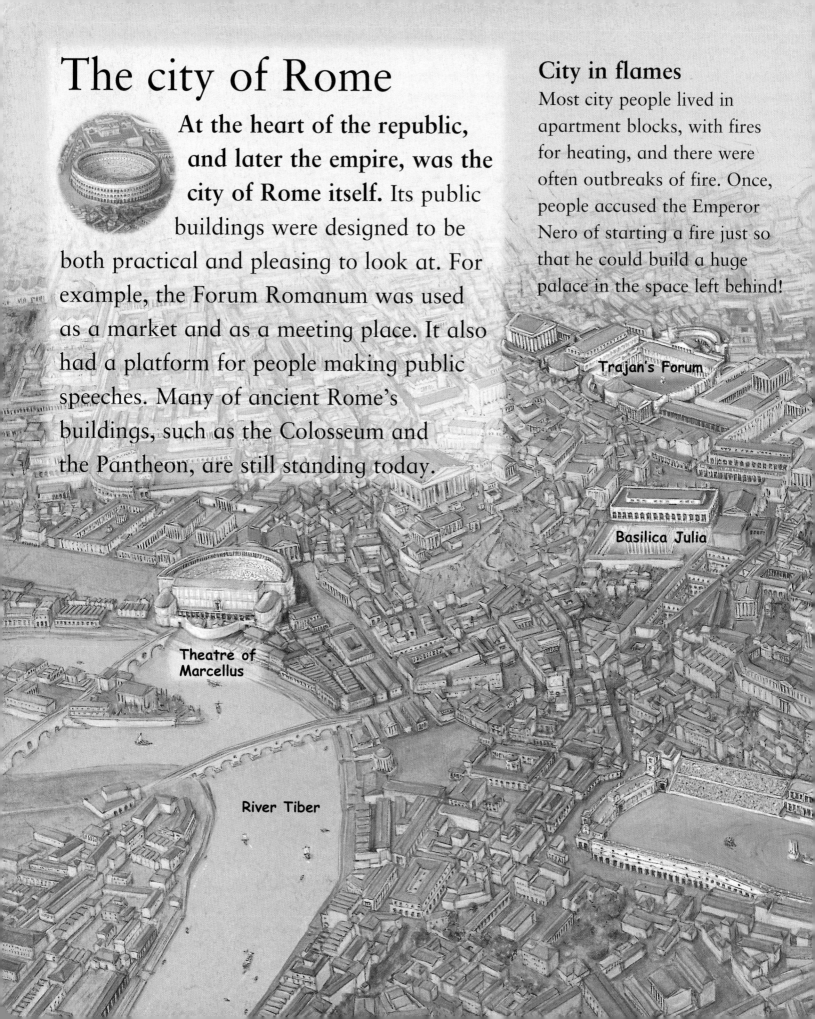

The city of Rome

At the heart of the republic, and later the empire, was the city of Rome itself. Its public buildings were designed to be both practical and pleasing to look at. For example, the Forum Romanum was used as a market and as a meeting place. It also had a platform for people making public speeches. Many of ancient Rome's buildings, such as the Colosseum and the Pantheon, are still standing today.

City in flames

Most city people lived in apartment blocks, with fires for heating, and there were often outbreaks of fire. Once, people accused the Emperor Nero of starting a fire just so that he could build a huge palace in the space left behind!

Trajan's Forum

Basilica Julia

Theatre of Marcellus

River Tiber

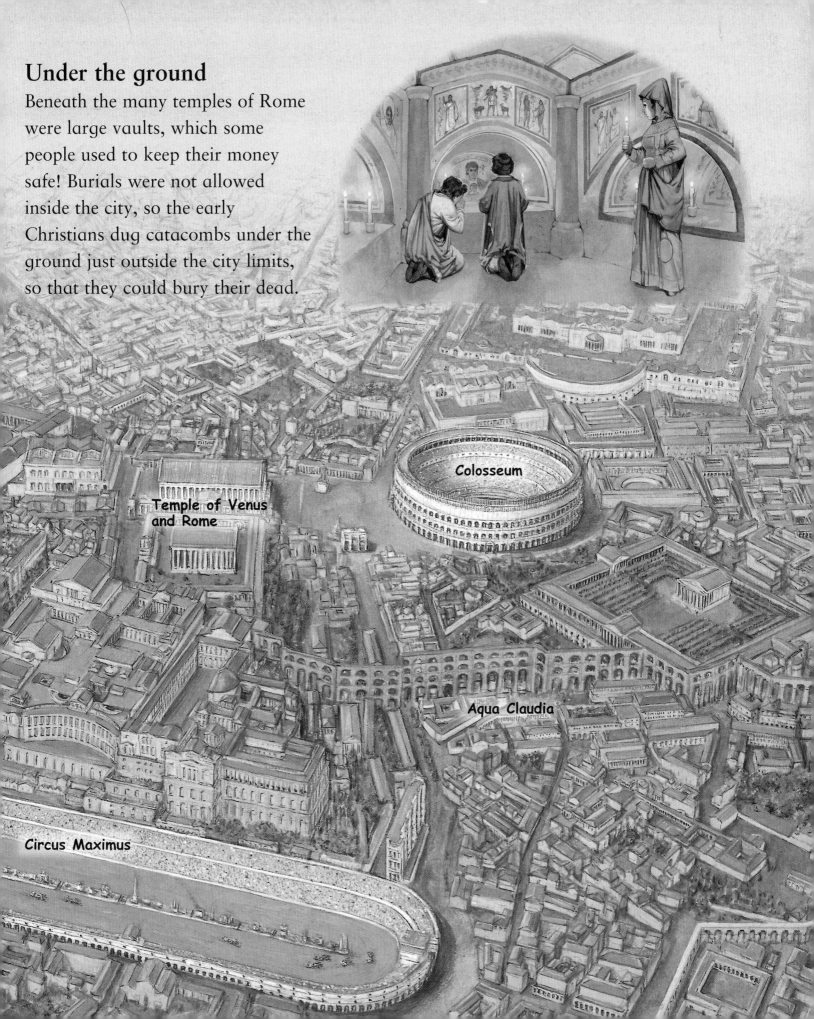

Under the ground

Beneath the many temples of Rome were large vaults, which some people used to keep their money safe! Burials were not allowed inside the city, so the early Christians dug catacombs under the ground just outside the city limits, so that they could bury their dead.

Colosseum

Temple of Venus and Rome

Aqua Claudia

Circus Maximus

Conquering new lands

Carthaginian
archers

The Roman republic had enemies on all sides. Some of the Latin cities formed a league to help each other fight the mountain tribes, and Rome joined it. By about 400BCE, Rome had a great deal of land and was the strongest city in the league. Even though other tribes, such as the Gauls, regularly attacked Rome, the republic continued to expand. By 264BCE, the Romans controlled all of Italy.

Auxiliary troops

The Roman army conquered many other lands, and also recruited local soldiers from the armies that they had fought. These soldiers, called auxiliaries, were useful because they knew the area well. They defended Rome's new borders.

Hannibal is humbled

From 264BCE, the Roman army fought a series of wars with the Carthaginians, from North Africa. In 218BCE, the Carthaginian general Hannibal invaded Italy with 35,000 men and over 30 elephants. He won battle after battle, but the Romans finally defeated him at Zama.

In 146BCE, Rome burned Carthage to the ground.

Roman legionaries

11

Building an empire

Roman borders continued to expand. However, fights among Rome's leaders soon turned into civil war. In 49BCE, Julius Caesar took control of Rome and in 44BCE he became dictator for life. But soon he was murdered and war broke out again. In 27BCE, Caesar's adopted son, Octavian, became the first Roman emperor, and was given the name Augustus.

Caesar on campaign

Julius Caesar was a brilliant politician and general. He fought many campaigns in Gaul and elsewhere from 58BCE to 49BCE, and he extended Rome's borders as far as the English Channel.

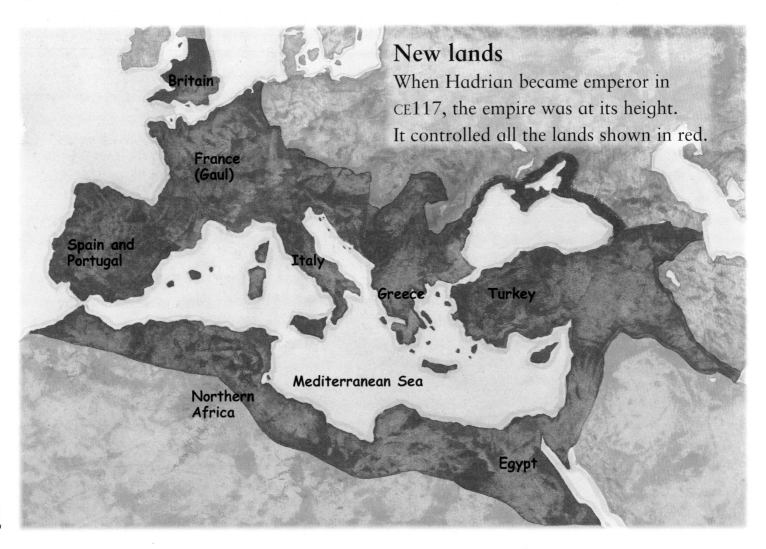

New lands

When Hadrian became emperor in CE117, the empire was at its height. It controlled all the lands shown in red.

Britain

France (Gaul)

Spain and Portugal

Italy

Greece

Turkey

Mediterranean Sea

Northern Africa

Egypt

12

The Romans and local tribes usually fought on foot.

Hadrian's wall

The Romans conquered Britain in CE43. Later, Emperor Hadrian built a great wall to help the army stop northern tribes from invading Britain. Some parts of the wall and its towers are still standing today.

Hadrian's wall is 117km long.

Controlling the tribes

Roman borders were constantly threatened by local tribes. Many of the tribes had so few weapons that they were unlikely to beat the mighty Roman army. However, they fought bravely and sometimes won astonishing victories.

13

Army life

 Rome's early army was made up of unpaid, untrained men. They were called up to fight when they were needed, and most had to provide their own weapons. By the 2nd century BCE, the army had become a highly trained, professional force. Each man was paid, and was given a set of weapons. When soldiers were not fighting, they spent much of their time training. Most were foot-soldiers but there were also soldiers on horseback, called the cavalry.

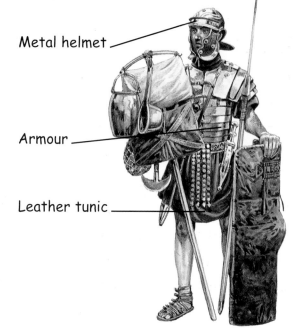

Metal helmet

Armour

Leather tunic

A legionary's weapons

Legionaries, or foot-soldiers, had a short sword for stabbing and a javelin for throwing. They also carried a large shield and wore metal armour for protection.

The tortoise

When approaching an enemy, groups of Roman soldiers often formed a tortoise shape, called a testudo. They held their shields over their heads and around the sides of the group. This formation helped to protect them from enemy missiles.

Military forts

In the early empire the Romans began to build permanent forts to protect their empire's borders. All the forts had the same plan, so when soldiers had to move from one to another it was very easy to find their way around the new fort.

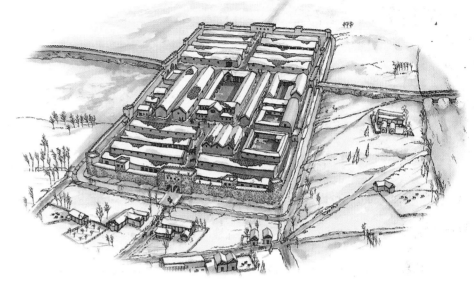

Cilurnum, a Roman military fort, was at Chester, in Britain.

Javelins made of iron and wood

Roman soldiers used shields made from wood and metal, covered in leather.

Daily life in Rome

For the richest families, life in ancient Rome was easy. They had large houses, good food and slaves to do their work for them. But because slaves did most of the work, paid jobs were difficult to find. Many ordinary people had no way of earning a living. Some Romans were so poor that they could not survive without help. Towards the end of the republic, the government regularly gave free corn to the poor of the city of Rome.

Trade

Some people earned money by trading. Ships brought trade goods from the Mediterranean area and beyond. These included basic items such as wool and corn, and luxuries such as amber.

A Roman merchant ship

Earning a living

Most people had to earn
a living to feed themselves and
their families. Some people made and
sold food, clothes or other goods. Others
provided services, such as secretarial work.

**Roman shops
sold all kinds of
everyday items.**

**Big ships could not sail
up the Tiber to Rome,
but had to deliver their
goods to Ostia, a large
seaport nearby.**

A slave auction

The rich Romans used
slaves to farm their land
and clean their houses. They
bought them at an auction
like the one shown here.
Some Romans were kind to
their slaves, and sometimes
even set the most loyal and
faithful ones free. However,
many treated their slaves
very badly, and beat them.

Slaves were sold at auctions.

17

In the home

Most Romans lived and worked in the country. People in cities and towns usually lived in blocks of flats, called insulae, with a few pieces of basic furniture. Rich families owned large homes, and often had a town house as well as a country villa. Roman villas were usually set in large grounds, which the owners farmed. A grand home often had fine mosaics and other decorations on the floors and walls.

Many teachers were Greek slaves.

A little learning

Boys from wealthy families were quite well educated. They learned how to read, write and count, either at home or in a school, called a ludus. Girls, however, usually only learned how to spin, weave and sew.

Rich people often owned a town house, like this one.

Hole in roof to let light in

Bedroom

Atrium

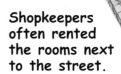

Shopkeepers often rented the rooms next to the street.

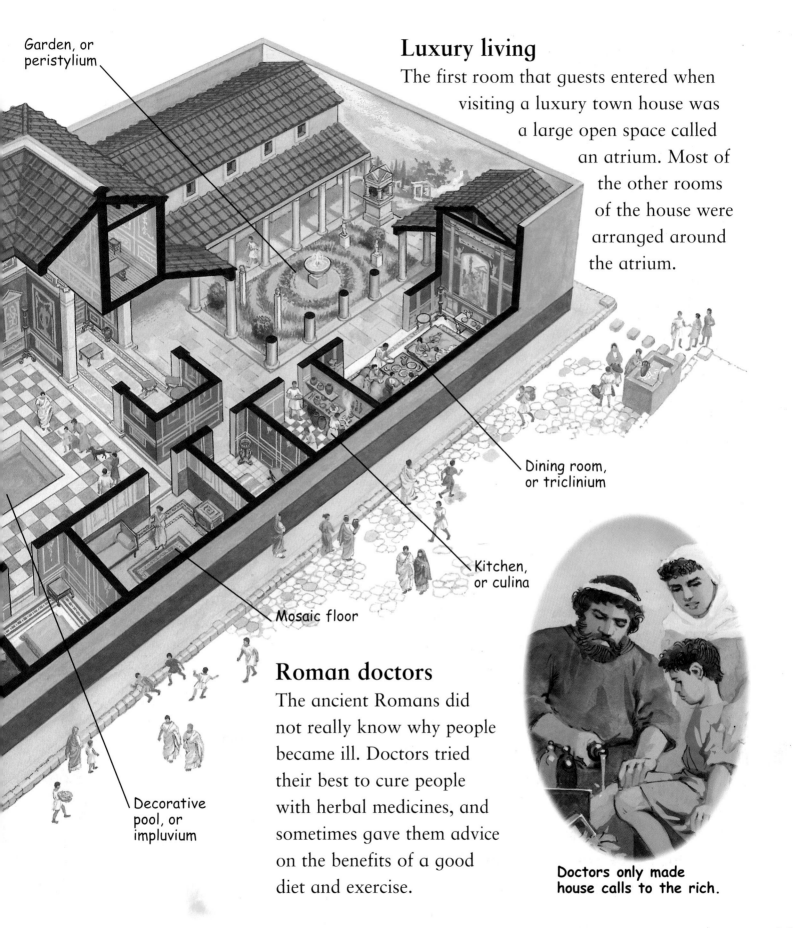

Garden, or
peristylium

Luxury living

The first room that guests entered when
visiting a luxury town house was
a large open space called
an atrium. Most of
the other rooms
of the house were
arranged around
the atrium.

Dining room,
or triclinium

Kitchen,
or culina

Mosaic floor

Decorative
pool, or
impluvium

Roman doctors

The ancient Romans did
not really know why people
became ill. Doctors tried
their best to cure people
with herbal medicines, and
sometimes gave them advice
on the benefits of a good
diet and exercise.

**Doctors only made
house calls to the rich.**

Time to spare

Citizens of ancient Rome had a lot of spare time. The normal working day began in the early morning, and ended at noon. There were about 100 days in the year when most people did not work at all. Rome's rulers provided many kinds of entertainment, and some of them were free, so that even poor people could have a good time!

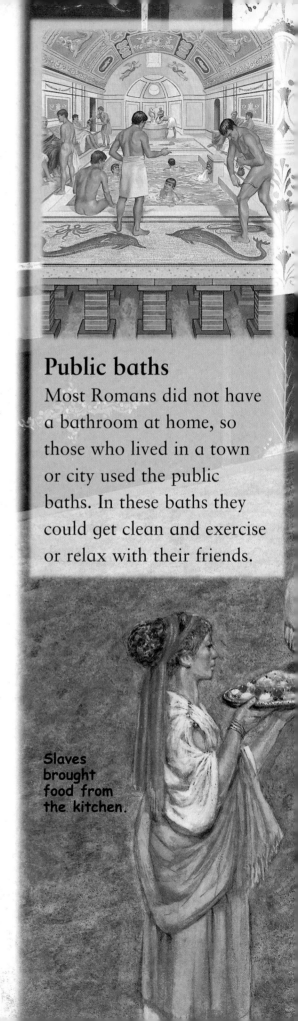

Public baths

Most Romans did not have a bathroom at home, so those who lived in a town or city used the public baths. In these baths they could get clean and exercise or relax with their friends.

At the theatre

Roman people loved going to the theatre. They laughed at comedies, and cried at tragedies. The actors wore masks and colourful robes so that the audience could recognize the characters even from the back row.

Slaves brought food from the kitchen.

Entertainers, such as musicians or clowns, amused the guests.

A feast fit for a king

Eating could be a big social event in Rome, especially for the rich. Guests lay on couches around low tables, and ate straight from the serving dishes. Noble families tried to impress each other by having the best dinner parties.

People usually ate with their fingers.

Gladiators and wild beasts

At the arena there were wild animal fights in the morning, and gladiator fights in the afternoon. The gladiators fought with various weapons, often to the death. However, a wounded gladiator could ask for mercy, and sometimes it was granted.

A myrmillon had a short sword and a rectangular shield.

A Thracian had a curved dagger and a small, square shield.

A retiarius had a trident and a net.

A Samnite had a short sword and a long, curved shield.

Sports and leisure

Sports in ancient Rome were different from those today. They were more dangerous, and many of the people who took part were forced to do so. Most of them were slaves, criminals or enemy soldiers. To begin with, gladiator fights and chariot races were only held on special days. But they were so popular that Rome's rulers decided to have them more often!

Spartacus

In the 1st century BCE, a Thracian soldier called Spartacus was sold as a gladiator. He escaped and formed a large army of slaves. They resisted many attacks by Roman troops, but were defeated when they invaded Rome.

A day at the races

At chariot races, teams of drivers, chariots and horses competed. They hurtled around the oval racetrack seven times, with chariots falling over, and horses and people getting hurt or even killed. The fans sometimes became so excited that they began fighting among themselves!

The Circus Maximus was the biggest racetrack in the empire, and larger than any sports stadium built since!

23

The fall of the empire

By the 4th century CE, the Roman empire was in serious trouble. Disease, hunger, rising prices, civil unrest and invasion all had a terrible effect. In CE395, the empire split permanently into two. The Western empire only lasted until CE476, when it was conquered by Odoacer, a Germanic warrior. The Eastern empire, known as the Byzantine empire, survived for almost another 1,000 years.

Emperor Constantine

By the time of Constantine in the 4th century CE, the empire had been split in two. Constantine reunited the two halves of the empire, but moved its capital from Rome to Byzantium, which he renamed Constantinople.

Vandals overrun Rome

The city of Rome had its own special fighting force, called the Praetorian guard. But when the Vandals, from northern Europe, invaded in CE455, the guardians were unable to stop them!

Constantinople topples

The Eastern empire survived until 1453, when Turkish Muslims laid siege to Constantinople. There were about ten times more attackers than defenders, and the city fell. The last part of the empire was defeated.

The Vandals ransacked Rome for several days, taking valuable objects, such as gold and bronze.

The legacy of Rome

Ancient Rome still affects our lives today.
The republican governments in the USA and France are based on the Roman republic, and the USA even has a Senate and senators. Many modern European languages, such as French and Spanish, are based on Latin, the language of the ancient Romans. Even the calendar that we use was invented during Julius Caesar's reign!

Roman aqueducts, which were built for carrying water, still stand all over Europe.

Romans building an aqueduct

Built to last

The Romans built things to last, and much of their work survives. Other people have copied the Roman style, and towns and cities all over the world have buildings like those of ancient Rome.

Building a Roman road

1 First, the road builders dug a trench and removed all the loose soil and rocks. This gave them a solid surface on which to work.

2 Then, the builders poured in layers of fine, dry earth and small stones. The road was highest in the middle to help drain away water.

3 The next layer contained a kind of concrete, made of broken stones and lime. This was followed by a layer of gravel or sand.

4 Finally, smooth, flat stone slabs were laid on top. The hard-wearing surface that they formed often lasted for many centuries.

Famous Romans

Many Romans were famous for being great soldiers or emperors, like these men on the right. But there were also Romans who became famous for other talents, such as acting, singing, writing or great sportsmanship!

Julius Caesar c.100-44BCE A dictator for life from 45BCE, and murdered in 44BCE.

Augustus 63BCE-CE14 The first emperor, who ruled wisely and improved the capital.

Hadrian CE76-138 An emperor who built great forts and walls to protect the empire.

Constantine the Great c.CE274-337 A Christian emperor who reunited the two halves of the empire.

Mount Vesuvius

The destruction of Pompeii

In CE79, a volcano called Mount Vesuvius erupted in a huge explosion. Buildings in the nearby city of Pompeii were destroyed, and many people and animals died. In the 18th century CE, archaeologists uncovering the city found that the ash had preserved many items perfectly.

Many objects, such as money, jewellery and food, were found at Pompeii.

Some of the buildings uncovered still had brightly coloured walls.

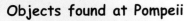
Objects found at Pompeii

A Roman gladiator's helmet

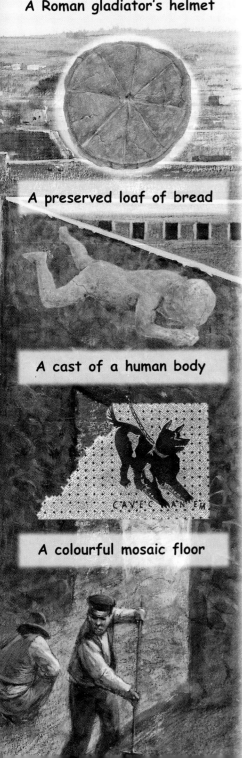
A preserved loaf of bread

A cast of a human body

A colourful mosaic floor

How do we know?

We know a great deal about ancient Rome from the writers of the time. Most of the original writing is lost, but in the late empire people began to make copies of the works of ancient Roman historians, poets and other writers. We can also learn from the work of archaeologists, who look at the remains of settlements and the items found there, and work out how people lived at the time.

Shipwrecks

On the ocean floor, marine archaeologists have discovered the remains of Roman ships. These can tell us what kinds of cargo they were carrying, such as the amphora, or container, above. We can also see how the ships were made, and how sailors lived.

Rome today

The city of Rome is the capital of modern Italy. It is the political and business centre of the nation, and is at the heart of tourism and culture. But in between the shops and modern offices, there are still many ancient buildings. Children play among the columns of the Pantheon, and cars drive around Rome's most famous arena – the Colosseum.

Ancient and modern

This picture shows part of Rome today. Over the years, people have stripped the valuable outer layers off some of the oldest buildings, to use for new structures. Pollution and traffic vibration have also badly damaged the old buildings.

The Colosseum

Glossary

amber Fossilised tree resin (sap), often used in jewellery.

amphora A container used for food, oil and other items.

archaeologist A person who studies ancient objects and the remains of ancient sites to find out how people lived.

archer A soldier who fights using a bow and arrow.

arena The space where gladiators and other entertainers performed for an audience.

auction A sale where goods are sold to the person willing to pay the highest price.

cast Something which forms in the space that is left by another object.

catacomb A place underground with many tunnels, where the early Christians living in ancient Rome buried their dead.

civil war A war fought between people of the same nation.

comedy A play that has a happy, or comic, ending.

dictator A ruler with total power over his people.

empire A group of nations, usually ruled by the leader of the strongest nation.

general An army officer in command of many soldiers.

gladiator A person, usually male, trained to fight in an arena to entertain an audience.

league A group of people who all work for the same purpose.

patrician The head of one of the richest families in ancient Rome.

plebeian Any free person in Rome who was not a patrician.

politician A person who works as part of the government of a country or nation.

pollution Car fumes and other toxic substances that can harm people, animals and buildings.

republic A nation whose rulers are elected by its people.

Senate The council of senators.

siege An attack in which armed forces surround a city or town.

temple A building where people go to worship their god, or gods.

toga A kind of robe, worn draped around the body.

tragedy A play that has a sad, or tragic, ending.

tribune A person elected by the plebeians to speak in council.

vault An underground room, often in a temple or bank, where people store important items.

veto The power to prevent others introducing a law or other rule.

Index